OUR SENSES

by Michèle Dufresne

Pioneer Valley Educational Press, Inc.

Your body can help you
to see, hear, smell, taste,
and touch things.

You can **see** with your eyes.

This apple looks good.

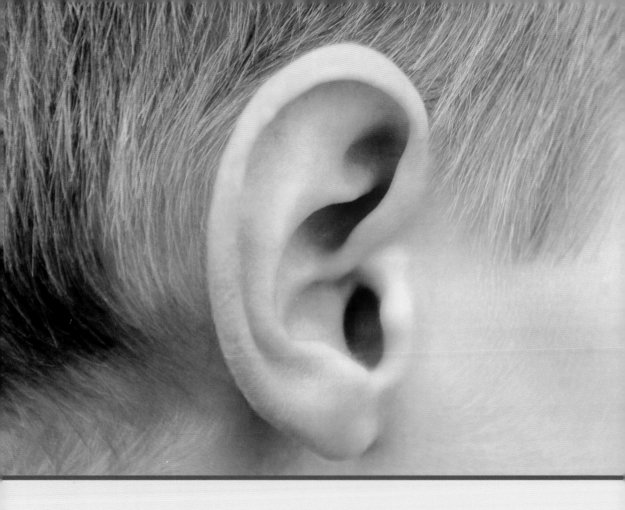

You can **hear** with your ears.

This music sounds good.

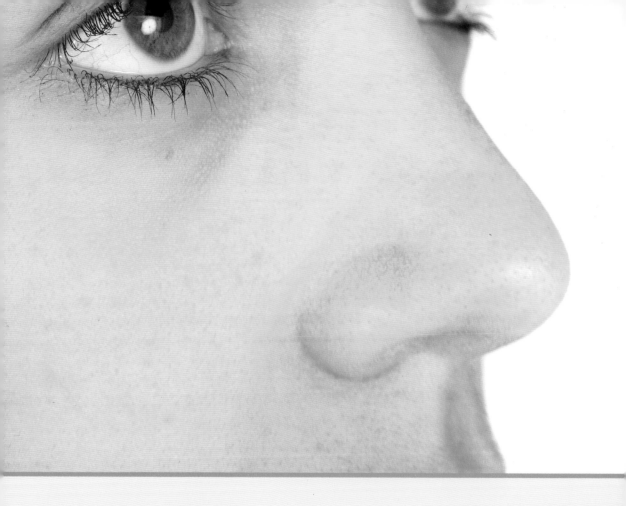

You can **smell** with your nose.

This flower smells good.

You can **taste** with your tongue.

This ice cream tastes good.

You can **touch** with your hand.

This kitten feels good.

Your body can help you to see, hear, smell, taste, and touch things.

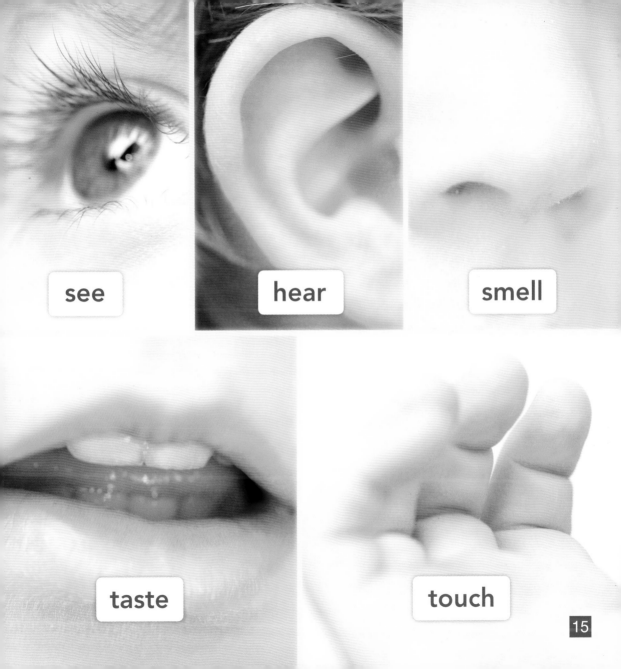

see

hear

smell

taste

touch

15

GLOSSARY

hear: to listen to

see: to look at

smell: to become aware of a scent or odor

taste: to try the flavor of something

touch: to feel gently